You Are Not Alone!
(I Promise)

The Journey of a Pansexual,
Gender-Fluid, Crossdresser

by

Robin Raynor

DORRANCE
PUBLISHING CO
EST. 1920
PITTSBURGH, PENNSYLVANIA 15238

Dorrance Publishing Co
585 Alpha Drive
Suite 103
Pittsburgh, PA 15238
Visit our website at www.dorrancebookstore.com

ISBN: 978-1-6461-0491-8
eISBN: 978-1-6461-0732-2

I would like to stress that I am not a licensed therapist. Any views or opinions that I may stress in this book are mine alone and do not reflect that of my publisher.

Special Thanks to Susan Hayatghib. If it weren't for you, I might not be here today. Also to everyone who has supported me on my wild and crazy journey.

CHAPTER ONE

Origins

Who am I? That is the eternal question, isn't it? Didn't Clark Kent ask that of Jor-El in *Superman* the movie? As for me specifically, I was born with the name Chang Sang Man, in what is known as South Korea today. Other than that, my origins remain a mystery to me to this day. Oh, sure, I can get an over-the-counter DNA test and easily find out more, but given my current budget and my lack of motivation to find out more about that part of my life, it's not going to happen anytime soon.

I was once asked by someone what my earliest memory is. It was being on the plane that took me from South Korea to the United States, where I was adopted by an American couple, Tom and Jill Caralyus, in Westchester County, New York. Not too long after that, I was renamed Eric John Caralyus and became an American citizen. Three years later, my family became complete when my sister Carrie Jo was born into the world.

I can remember having a very happy early childhood, and being loved by my family very much. So when and why did things start to go downhill for me? I have no idea. It was probably when I was exposed to life outside my home, when reality came crashing down on me very hard. Both Tom and Jill were raised Catholic, and of course they wanted me and Carrie to be the same way. So it was during my early school years that I began my rocky relationship with the Catholic religion.

It was in the first grade, in St. Joseph's School, that I met someone who would teach me how cruel people could be. Her name was Sister Christine. I could never understand why she disliked me so much to this day, but I vividly remember things that she did to me, like not letting me eat with the other students during lunch, or frequently keeping me after school to bang erasers or do some kind of other punishment cleanup like I was a prisoner of some sort. And I remember that she was always yelling at me for something.

At first, Tom and Jill thought I was the problem, that I simply wasn't applying myself or doing enough. I know I should've said something to them sooner, but the way they talked down on me, frequently in a tone of disappointment, convinced me that I was the problem. It wasn't until some of our neighbors, whose kids were in my class, spoke out against Sister Christine to them that they realized who the real culprit was.

Jill told me that when she found out, she chased down Sister Christine, screaming to her the whole time until she found a way to lock herself in some place to get away from Jill. After that, in one of the few times that they would in their life, they apologized to me and told me that I wasn't going back to that school. I guess I naively thought that life was going to get better after that, but reality was not done with me by a longshot.

Public school in that area was very much a mostly white, middle-class area, and the kids could be very cruel towards those who they thought they could pick on for whatever their reasons. I remember being called names like "Chink" or "Whap" by some of the kids (I remember one kid calling me a Nigger even). Or they would tease me by pulling the ends of their eyes and chanting, "Me Chinese, me Chinese…." I can't even remember the number of times I had my hair pulled or was punched. Not everyone was like that, but sadly, many were. Also because I was that "easy target," I was bullied by both genders for many of my early years. I can remember many days feeling cursed that I wasn't thin and white.

I truthfully think that it would've been way worse without the presence of a good friend that I made through those years. Ironically enough, he started out as my bully early on. We didn't become friends until we went on an overnight school trip, and had to share the same room with two others. These days, we recently reconnected and remain good friends today.

Every day, when I would go home at the end of school, I would tell Tom and Jill about everything that happened there. They would just tell me to "buck up," "ignore them," or later on "man up" (whatever that means). The only time they would do anything was when the bullies left marks on me. As I got older, however, those bullies wouldn't be the only ones leaving their mark on me.

It's hard to pinpoint a specific time or event when it started to happen, but Jill became physically and mentally abusive towards me and Carrie when she would lose her temper. It started off with spankings (which was considered normal in the 70s and 80s) and evolved into numerous slaps across the face, and one time led to me being whipped by my own belt. It was because of that, that for many years into my early adulthood, I didn't wear a belt because of the memories it brought back.

It unfortunately didn't stop there, as another time she balled up her fists and hit me repeatedly in the rib area, leaving me a quivering mess. Many years later, I would learn that Carrie was not spared either. She recalled a time when Jill shoved her head into a wall, among other things.

Why did I never reach out to another adult, or call the police or something? The truth was that Jill was also the master manipulator, and fooled many, many people for years into believing that she was a caring, upstanding mother. You also may ask where Tom was for all this time. I suspect he knew some of what was going on, but he didn't have the stones to confront Jill. Likewise, there were some who knew what kind of person she was, but they didn't want to get involved and they did nothing.

You may ask what kept me from suicide after reading all this. Truthfully, I thought about it several times, but never went through with it. I don't know what saved me exactly—hope, divine intervention, maybe a stubborn part of me that refused to give up. All I know is thankfully I'm still here today.

So why be so candid and revealing after years of silence, you may ask? Well, I'm not doing this for money, or to ask for sympathy, or anything like that. I am simply telling all of this to give you, the reader, an idea of what shaped me into the person I am today. You're also probably wondering where things like crossdressing, gender fluidity, and pansexuality, as I've advertised, come in. I promise, if I've piqued your interest and you want to read on, it will all fall into place.

Robin Raynor

CHAPTER TWO

Early Crossdressing and Feelings of Sexuality

A lot of people I've compared notes with about their first experience with their feminine sides are all different. Some say that they dressed in their mother's clothes and shoes as a kid. Others say it was the first time they dressed as a woman for Halloween. As for me, I actually fell into crossdressing by accident.

I always admired how women would dress pretty, but my curiosity was piqued the first time when I was five or six years old. My mother's stockings were drying on a towel rack, and I wondered to myself, *Why do women wear those?* So really, just to be silly, I put them on. The feelings I experienced next were unlike anything I'd previously felt, or have since then.

I felt all tingly in my legs. Although I didn't know it at the time, I was feeling very sexy in those stockings. I realized, however, that I couldn't stay behind that locked door for too long, as my parents probably would've wondered what exactly I was doing in there. So I reluctantly took them off, replaced them where they were, and went off to bed (though I was too excited to sleep for a while after that).

While all our bedrooms were in the same vicinity, and we were sharing the same bathroom, I did it time and time again to recapture that feeling. My fun came to a screeching halt, however, as my parents moved their bedroom downstairs and we no longer shared the same bathroom about a year or two later. To say I was disappointed was an understatement. I thought I would never regain that feeling ever again. Fortunately for me, however, I was wrong.

My next notable experience came when I was seven or eight years old. I remember telling my parents that I wanted to be Pinocchio for Halloween that year. To complete the costume that they made for me, Jill bought me a pair of brown tights. You can only imagine my euphoria as that old familiar feeling came back as I tried them on. Leading up to Halloween, I snuck putting them on again a couple of times, when I was supposed to be sleeping. After Halloween, however, Jill threw the tights away, and I was left feeling empty again.

When I hit puberty (which is a very awkward stage as it is), it was compounded by the fact that I found women's clothes more appealing than ever. Yes, I liked the way they looked on women, but I strangely began to imagine what I would look like in them. I believe that this was also the time when I began to wonder what it was like to be a girl. Let's face it, however; as I mentioned, I had God-fearing parents. To say that I didn't feel comfortable relaying my feelings to them was an understatement!

Also around this time, I was curious how other types of women's clothes would feel on me. Eventually, I tried on Jill's bras, panties, dresses, and shoes. Again, I felt very sexy, but this time around I understood the feeling better. Eventually, however, I was found out. Jill never directly caught me in the act, but would occasionally notice when her things were out of place. I would always get an earful after getting caught by her.

I believe that part of the reason my parents sent me to my first shrink was to try to "fix" me. If that was part of their plan, however, it didn't work. No matter how many times I would get busted, I would constantly be looking for an opportunity to do it again. Despite the feelings it would give me every time I did it, however, I felt very much alone. My family was no help, and realistically trying to explain such feelings and sensations

Robin Raynor

to any of my peers was not really an option, considering that most of them thought I was strange as it was.

So how did I deal with all of this at this young age, you may ask? The truth was, was that I didn't. I just did what my parents always did, and shoved it deep down within my psyche like a good little boy, and tried to go on, business as usual, as they say.

There was another reason that I did all that: because of our religious beliefs. All my life, I can say that I never truly knew how my parents felt about the LGBTQ community, but deep down, I think that they always believed that people like that went to Hell. It would certainly explain why they worked so hard to keep me "normal" in everybody's eyes (God's included). It would be several years until I felt free to explore that side of myself again.

Meanwhile, at a time when most children thought the opposite sex was "icky," I had my first crush on a girl. As usual, I tried telling my parents the feelings I was experiencing (a giddy, tingly like feeling), but as usual, they blew me off, telling me that I was too young to have feelings like that. This was the first time I had feelings for girls.

As for guys, I didn't have many man crushes during my education years. I do remember, however, that I developed feelings for an actor named John Schneider at a young age (he was on a show called *The Dukes of Hazzard*). I couldn't explain my feelings towards him at that time. I guess that I reasoned that I felt that way because I thought he was cool. That's the way I would also explain most of my future man crushes.

As I was growing up, I was frequently told that I would grow up, fall in love, and marry the right woman. Why wouldn't I believe it? After all, I did like girls. I also grew up in a small town where LGBTQ presence was virtually nonexistent. I wouldn't learn anything about people who fit in that category until I saw some in TV and movies.

If I had to pin down the first gay man I ever saw, it was probably actor Paul Lindy (even though I didn't know it at the time). I don't think I saw a lesbian until I watched my first porno movie years later. The first trans person I saw was the infamous trans woman who had been a "Bond babe," from the famous 007 James Bond movie series. As far as bisexuality or pansexuality, I wouldn't learn about those until I was much older.

All I realized during my childhood, however, was that I seemingly fit "the mold," and I was content with that for many years. I never would've guessed that I would one day break out of that mold.

CHAPTER THREE

Higher Education and Mental Illness?

When I was in my early teens, I met another person who would start out as my bully and, for a time, would become my friend. I learned a lot about sex from him because Tom and Jill were too timid to educate me properly. Sadly, I was also molested by him once. We were alone in my room, and all of a sudden, something came over him and he gave me an evil-like look.

He told me to take off my pants and underwear. Because he was much, much stronger than me physically, I was too scared to say no. He then dropped his pants and underwear, and was fully erect. He shoved me to the ground, and began to ram his penis into my scrotum several times while holding me down, until all of a sudden, he stopped. He said he didn't know what came over him, and begged me not to tell anyone. Truthfully, I was too embarrassed and humiliated to say anything, so for years, I kept silent and thought it was all my fault.

After graduating junior high school, I was faced with a choice by my parents. To go to public or a Catholic, private high school. Naively thinking that I would get a fresh start, I chose the private school. Basically, it was a case of same old crap, different school. After my first year there, it became obvious that I had to join a clique to get through the next three years.

So in my sophomore year, I met an ally. Someone who didn't care about "fitting in" or any of that stuff. So for the rest of my high school years, people considered me a rebel and metalhead. Thankfully, with the advent of that, I managed to make some good friends who had the same mentality as me.

It was also around this time that I was experiencing symptoms of a condition that I was likely born with. The medical term is Schizoaffective Disorder; basically you see and/or hear things that aren't there. I experienced it a little when I was younger, but for the most part, it was very minor.

One notable exception was when I came home from school one day. I want to say that I was eight or so, but I truthfully don't remember. All I remember was hearing several voices talking in my head at once, and no one else was around. I became paralyzed with fear and started bawling. It didn't stop until Jill arrived home. She ran over and asked me what was wrong. Having heard awful stories about how mental hospitals kept you sedated 24/7 and away from regular society, I made an excuse (I think I said that one of my story records scared me).

As if the Schizoaffective Disorder wasn't enough, I also began to experience depression during my high school years. Given what I've revealed so far, you can only imagine how much of a struggle it was to get through a day. Now imagine occasionally seeing the WWE wrestler the Undertaker towering over you through some of your darkest moments. It was around this time that I first started to think of suicide frequently.

I also at this time vividly remember this one individual who many in the school thought was gay (myself included). I truly don't know if he was or not, but he kinda fit the part. These days, I curse myself because I gave in to mob mentality and joined in the movement to hassle him. If I had the chance to today, I would say that I'm sorry and would beg his forgiveness.

Somehow I managed to make it through and graduate high school (barely). I had big plans. I wanted to take a year off of school and find some people to backpack around Europe with, to "find myself," so to speak. But, being a traditional couple, Tom and Jill wanted me to go to college right away. Truthfully, I should've stood up to them, but at the time, I didn't have the stones to defy them. So, I went to a two-year college for forestry (actually ended up spending three years there because of changing my major a couple of times and trying to earn two two-year degrees). It was also there that I met a girl who would have a significant impact on me.

She was an RA (Resident Assistant), and at first, because of this, I viewed her as the enemy (as I did most figures in authority at that time). It wasn't until one night, when I went on a real bender, that I began to change my views on her. I was told that during that drunken stupor that she spent hours at my bedside, making sure I was all right. On another occasion, I fondly remember her giving me support once when I was crying because Carrie told me that Tom and Jill were constantly fighting.

She was only there that one semester, because it was her last one. The night before we all left to go home for that semester, I drew a picture on a homemade card and told her a heartfelt goodbye. Before going to bed, she knocked on my door, tearful, and said goodbye to me. Then, she surprised me by giving me a great big hug. Because I never experienced that much sincere emotion before, I was dumbfounded. I just stood there, not knowing what to do, and that was the last that I saw of her.

The following semester, because she was gone, my drinking began to spiral out of control. It started out as a weekend thing, but very quickly escalated to every day. I almost failed out after my second semester, but I worked hard over that summer and managed to bring up a failing grade to a passing one, via community college.

Although grade wise I eventually did a big turnaround, I began to develop bad anxiety around this time (especially during school breaks, because I was usually one of the last ones to leave). Really, the only silver lining was that I fell hard for someone around this time.

She was a cafeteria worker. She didn't have supermodel looks, but her eyes were so calming and friendly. I remember days when I was completely depressed, and all she had to do was look into my eyes, smile, and say hi, and I immediately felt better. She just made me feel good about myself. I took a chance and told her how I felt about her in a note. But later on, she let me down easy, and explained that she was already seeing somebody. I was greatly disappointed, but eventually managed to get through it.

There was another person I met in junior college at this time, however, who would greatly shape me during my time there. She was the learning disability counselor. She was always very happy and optimistic, and it was infectious. I truthfully don't know if I could've made it through junior college without her help and support. And truthfully, I always had a feeling that she knew me better than I knew myself.

As my time wound down there, I would do something that I regret to this day; I applied to a four-year college, never dreaming that I would be accepted, but I was. All my peers, instructors, and even my parents gave me their full support. So after I graduated junior college, I tried my hand at going all the way to Colorado to continue my education. Why do I regret such a decision? Let me explain.

My parents' way of dealing with a tough problem was denial, and shoving it deep inside themselves. I unfortunately did the same thing for many years. But because I did it so much up to that point, my mental condition, depression, and anxiety were beginning to spill out. It got so bad that I became super paranoid (to the point where I was afraid to leave my dorm room). As a result, I was in and out of mental hospitals because I began to feel suicidal again. It was also because of this that I eventually flunked out of college.

Worse yet, because I was having episodes where I would pass out. The college didn't understand what was going on with me, and I was told to leave the campus and never come back. After bouncing around in places and hospitals for a while, Tom flew out and asked me to come home. Truthfully, I didn't trust him when he promised that things would be different from now on, but I really had no other place to go, and I naively and desperately wanted to believe him. So I went home.

I should've trusted my first instinct, because in a nutshell, nothing good changed at all. If anything, things had become worse. Jill was as difficult as ever, and once again, Tom was no help to me at all. In fact, he took my vehicle off his insurance, and insisted that I pay for my own from now on. I didn't exactly have a problem with that, but when I got my first bill with Tom's go-to insurance, they wanted over $200 a month, and here I was only making minimum wage at the time (I believe that it was $4.25 at that time)!

I guess what I really resented at that time was that Tom and Jill were insensitive to my conditions (denial again), neither one ever took any time to prepare me for the outside world in any way, and I guess that I was more than ticked that Tom insisted that I pay rent for living in the house I grew up in.

It made me a bitter person. For spite, I never paid him any rent money (which I admit was wrong). I sunk every dollar I made into the local strip club, and never stayed at home, except to sleep. Ultimately, my behavior was so out of control that one night, Tom gave me an ultimatum. Basically, I had to do things his way from now on, or find somewhere else to live. It was at that moment that I finally grew a backbone and decided that even no home was better than the current situation. So I told him that I would move out tomorrow.

So early the next day, I loaded up my truck with my things. All Tom said to me the whole time was, "You're a very stubborn person, Eric," and "Where will you go?" That was it. I said goodbye to my sister, but not to either parent, and drove away, never to return.

I ended up staying with a coworker for a while, but she made it clear that it was only a temporary situation. While there, I constantly contemplated what to do next. All I knew was that I didn't want to stay in New York. Then, inspiration hit me in the form of a music video.

I don't remember the band, or even the name of the song. All I remember is the opening lyric of the song, which went: "I'm going down to Southern California...." So I said to myself, "Hmmm... Southern California, Los

Angeles, that sounds cool...." So I sold my vehicle, and took a seasonal job to pay for my plane ticket. Then, on December 31st, 1995, I said goodbye to New York, and my old life.

CHAPTER FOUR

The Birth of Robin

On January 1st, 1996, I stepped off a plane in Los Angeles, CA, with no idea with what I was going to do with myself. This was before the age of Smartphones, so I was a total babe in the woods. I had enough money to stay in a motel for a couple of days, but I ran into a roadblock while trying to open a bank account with an out-of-state cashier's check. Worse still, when I did find a bank that would, they told me that it would take two weeks to verify the funds!

Two weeks on the mean streets of L.A. with no food, money, or shelter?! At that point, I knew that I'd get eaten alive. I didn't exactly have a backup plan, but it seemed like my only viable option was to try and make contact with an old college friend. So I used all the money I had left, and eventually found her. Her and her family were so key to helping me establish residency in CA, and I don't think I ever thanked them properly.

After that, I bounced around a little as far as my living situation (was even homeless for a short time, but not jobless). It was at one of my jobs that a coworker offered me a place to live (her garage) for cheap. While living there, I began to develop those old feelings of wanting to look and dress like a woman again. With no Tom and Jill to stop me this time, I decided to fully explore this side of myself.

Even though I was working, I wasn't making a lot of money at that time, so I literally had to buy a complete outfit one item at a time. I slowly, but surely did so, and when the time came to buy a wig, I splurged a bit to get it. Next, I waited for a day when my landlord and her children would be out of the house for a bit. Then, I shaved off all my facial and body hair. When I got out of the shower, the air on my newly shaved skin felt heavenly, so I quickly made my way back to my room to get dressed up.

The feeling of women's panties against my skin was very exciting (I never felt that way putting any underwear on)! When I put on my stockings, that old familiar sensation came back in droves! I put on my top, skirt, and shoes, and felt transformed into whole different person seemingly! I remember bits of excitement, curiosity, and wonder as I slipped my wig on for the first time!

When I was done, I looked at myself in the mirror for the first time like that, and couldn't believe what I was seeing! It was me, yet it wasn't at the same time! After several minutes of admiring myself, however, I had a sinking feeling. I thought to myself, *Oh my God! I'm probably the only person in the world that feels this way! I'm a freak!!* Still, I kept everything on until I knew when my landlord and her kids were coming home.

A couple of days after my first "coming out," I still had no idea where I was going with my newfound look. Then, just at random, I was thumbing through the free local paper one day, and came upon an ad for a new store called "Crossers," a store that catered to crossdressers. Imagine my relief when I realized that I wasn't the only one in the world. I made it a priority to find this store when I had time to myself.

On the day I was looking for it, it was a total nightmare to find! It was in a part of San Jose that I didn't know well at all. Even though I had a cellphone, Smartphones were still a little ways off, so it wasn't much help, except when I would call the store to see if I was getting any closer. Eventually, in the late afternoon of that day, I found it! Imagine my embarrassment, however, when I realized that I left my money at home!

The place was run by a kind woman who I would come to regard as the supportive mother figure I never had growing up. She took mercy on me that crazy day, and even let me change into my women's clothes for a while while I got to know her. It was also during that visit that she asked me what my "fem" name was (kind of like my alter ego when I was dressed up, sort of like a superhero). I had never really considered one when I did my thing for the first time. So on a spur of the moment, I said it was Jennifer.

A day after that, however, I said to myself, "There's hundreds of Jennifers out there." I then decided that I wanted a name that was a little more unique. Inspiration hit me when I was reading a *Batman* comic book. His sidekick, Robin, resonated within me. Upon further reflection, I realized that Robin could be a boy or girl's name! So from that point on, my "fem" persona was Robin (thankfully, the name stuck among those who knew what I was doing)! Little did I know that years later, I would change that to my legal name.

Even though I didn't wear any makeup, or pluck my eyebrows at that time, I was still surprisingly passable, and even got brave enough to venture out of the house dressed every so often at night. I never considered either before, until one time when I was having sex with a call girl and she asked me afterwards why I didn't do either. It was that girl who inspired me to complete my look.

These days, anyone can go on YouTube and find out how to do a decent makeover or proper plucking. Back in the late 90s, however, the internet was still very much in its infancy. So I learned what I did by buying some women's magazines. It was through those that I found and perfected the look that I still have to this day.

It was also around this time that I began to change my views on gay people. I met this one at my first job in CA. I realized that I really had two options. I could try to find another job, or I could try to get along with this person. Being that it had taken me a while to find that job, I opted for the latter. I'm glad that I did in retrospect. He was a nice and professional manager, and he always treated me with dignity and respect. He even offered me a nice, new job when he jumped ship to a well-known hotel chain. I should've taken his offer, but for whatever reasons at the time, I didn't.

Although things seemed to be coming together for me, the next ten years would prove to be anything but easy.

CHAPTER FIVE

The Next Stage

For the longest time, I was into the world of superheroes and comics. I guess I was always fascinated with their ability to be two entirely different people. For many years, I did this too. Like many of them are portrayed, I sometimes felt lost (it felt like I was searching for who the real me was). It played a big part in me "purging" for the first time.

For those who don't know this trans term, it's when you throw out all your womanly possessions and vow to live your life as a "normal," heterosexual man (or woman, if you reverse the principles for cis women). I remember one friend said she did this by "symbolically" burning them all in a metal drum. To any trans person, no matter where you are on your journey, my advice if you get these feelings is to ignore them!

Odds are that you are not being true to yourself, and at some point you will most likely regret it (if that's not good enough motivation, think of all the money you will spend trying to replace said items! Believe me, it adds up.). But know most of all that your feelings will never completely go away, and will come back sooner or later. This is a lesson I had to learn the hard way, being guilty of having done it twice in my lifetime.

A lot of those feelings were also fueled by the fact that I was frequently harassed whenever I went out as my fem self. It got so bad that in later years, I wouldn't go out at all for a while. Thankfully, however, at least in CA, attitudes are very different nowadays. If I had to guess, I think my general build gives me away (I am 5'7" without high heels, and a little stocky. On the flip side, I can pass as a full-figured woman.). The only place I felt safe to express myself that way for a while was the city (San Francisco).

Meanwhile, for the next ten years, I changed jobs and living spaces a couple of times. Each time I moved, I would struggle and adjust my dual life so that I could find a happy balance. I became pretty good at keeping my fem identity a secret from those around me. If anything gave me away, it was probably my eyebrows (which I kinda tend to overpluck). Even then, very few people noticed or cared.

At this one job, I met someone who would forever change my views on gay people and the LGBTQ community forever. At first, I had no idea he was gay, until some of my female coworkers told me. I couldn't believe it at first. A gay man who liked comics, *Star Wars,* and *Star Trek* and wasn't flamboyant? I thought he was an all-right guy, and like I mentioned, he changed my views forever. We were friends until he was unceremoniously fired.

Shortly after my second purge, I would be blindsided by something that I had been ignoring for many years: my overall mental health. Remember how I dealt with issues like that in my life? How I would ignore them, and shove them deep down in my psyche?

It was because of that that I was involved in an unfortunate incident at my job, where I lost my temper and hit someone because he was provoking me. Because I had great respect for my boss at the time, I owned up to it before he found out on his own. Ultimately, this led to my dismissal of that job.

Things only got worse from there. It was 2007, at a time when the economy was at an all-time low, so I couldn't find a new permanent job at all.

Months later, cold, hard reality came crashing down on me as I realized that soon I was going to be homeless and penniless. The mental health issues that I had ignored for years came flooding out, and no matter how hard I tried, I couldn't stop them. This eventually led to feelings of hopelessness and suicidal ideation again.

Then one night, I got up for work at my temporary job, and at one point glanced at my kitchen knife. Thoughts about using it to slit my wrists came into my head. I even got as far as picking it up and positioning it. Then, believe it or not, I was saved by my mental illness. I began to hear several voices in my head telling me to do it (kill myself), and all of a sudden, I became more scared of them than dying.

I left and locked up my apartment, went into a nearby parking lot, and called 911 on myself. A policeman quickly came and after and asked me some questions, then delivered me to EPS (Emergency Psychiatric Services).

From there, I had two consecutive hospital stays (ironically, the second one happened when the first hospital let me out a little too soon and I was being assessed by a nearby mental health clinic). It was before my second one that a counselor saved my life and had me returned to another hospital. It was a good thing, because I probably wasn't thinking clearly still. Unfortunately for me, I never got a chance to properly thank her.

It was during this trying time that I realized how much of a destructive path I was taking in life with my skewed way of thinking. It was also during this time that for the first time, I began to accept my mental health issues and my fem side. I also realized that I certainly didn't want to live in denial like my parents did anymore, so I listened to and took in everything they told me in both hospital stays. After I was finally done with hospitals, I began to slowly but surely start my road to recovery and acceptance of myself.

CHAPTER SIX

Finding My Place in this World

Atfter my second hospital stay, the people in charge there got me into what's known as a crisis residential home. If you've never heard of one before, it's kinda like a board-and-care home, except that it's more structured, having you attend five groups a day during the week. It was a place I could go temporarily instead of an extended hospital stay. (It was also good for me because it kinda eased me back into society instead of chucking me in the deep end and seeing if I'd sink or swim.)

I went from a short-term one to a longer-term one over the next year, and learned much about managing my mental illness symptoms. Also during my stays, various doctors (psychiatrists) experimented with different medications and doses of them.

Over the course of the next two years, I bounced around a couple of board-and-care homes. By 2009, however, I was sick of that environment (most likely because I was finally starting to stabilize mentally). So later that year, I finally decided to strike out on my own again. I rented a room from a couple, and even decided to try out an old dream I had when I was younger: becoming an animator.

I was always fascinated from an early age on how to make a still image seemingly move. Although I learned the basics of art, and many of the classic and modern techniques of 2-D animation (which was what initially caught my interest), it was required that I learn more. I had to learn aspects of 3-D animation, and countless editing software as well (Photoshop, Flash, Maya, and After Effects, to name a few).

Also that year, I began to seriously question my sexuality. I suspected for years that I was bisexual, but could never realize it for myself. So I sought out a professional's help. After taking a series of tests, she told me that I was indeed bisexual. I don't remember taking the news too well at first, and it would take many years to accept that part of me.

Eventually, a few years into my schooling, I ran into a new problem. At that time, I was splitting my time between a part-time job and school. My hats off to those amazing individuals who can balance a full-time job (or maybe two), going to school, and somehow raising a family, but I was not one of those people. I needed the job, because my disability benefits alone weren't enough. As a result of putting in some long hours at work, my grades began to slip more than I wanted them to.

I knew I could no longer keep up with both, and as much as I wanted to quit my job and devote myself completely to my studies, I realistically couldn't do that. So in 2014, I withdrew from school for good. Soon after, I also changed my job again, because realistically, dishwashing is really not a viable option for someone in their 40s (in the long term). I returned to a pharmacy store company that I had previously worked for and became an overnight clerk (which I do to this day).

So you might be wondering where my trans journey took me around this time. Well, after I struck out on my own again, I bought a complete women's outfit, shoes, and a wig (just in case I had the courage and opportunity to put them on again). Throughout all the places that I lived, I always made sure to take it with me.

Also in 2014, when I left school, that also meant that I had to leave student housing (which was shutting down anyway). During an online search for apartments, I actually found one that I could afford! Upon going there to get an application, I found out it was a Government-funded affordable apartment complex (that I thankfully qualified for).

I was also fortunate that I was able to move in three months later (and that was with no waiting list). Being that I was on my own again, I was free to get dressed up whenever I wanted! So I slowly began to expand my wardrobe. Even though I did this, I was still very much afraid to go outside dressed up again. I casually brought this up to a counselor that I was seeing at that time. She encouraged me to give it another try, citing that attitudes were different in CA from even ten years ago.

I was skeptical, but decided to give it another go one day. I got dressed up in a casual outfit (nice top, blue jeans, and sneakers), put on my full makeup and wig, and went out to a nearby store. I was pleasantly surprised as no one said anything bad to me, or even gave me a dirty look. Every subsequent time I did it gave me more confidence to do it again and again. These days, I don't even give it a second thought.

Also around this time, I learned a new term, "pansexuality." Simply put, it's when a person cares little about what a person looks like (gender and lifestyle wise), and falls for them because of their personality. Although this is how I currently identify myself, I still sometimes say that I'm bisexual to some people for simplicity's sake. I also learned the term "Gender Fluid;" which in my case means that sometimes I identify as male and other times I identify as female.

Also during these years, I changed a couple of things about my lifestyle. I finally decided to be true to myself in the respect that I no longer reserved dressing up just once a week to satisfy my urges (maybe throwing myself a bone is a better way to put it). Now I get dressed up whenever I feel like it. I also admitted to myself that I liked wearing women's clothes more than men's. As a result, I drastically reduced my male wardrobe, and no longer wear men's underwear (it's ladies' all the way, all the time for me now).

The good news doesn't stop there. When I finally created a Facebook account, I reconnected with some old family and friends. Not too much later, I publicly came out on the site, having finally accepted who I really was. I lost some family doing this after just reconnecting with them, but mostly everyone I know have been very supportive. Neither Tom or Jill were alive when I did this (I learned Tom died a couple of years ago, and Jill died not too long after. Both died from cancer.), but I'm not sorry about that at all. Neither probably would've taken it well anyways.

Although I hope that Jill has found a nice spot in Hell, I regret not having the courage to patch things up with Tom. He really wasn't a bad guy, just a lousy parent.

Another great bit of news is that I was recently allowed the option to come in "dressed" while working at my job (it wasn't a huge shock to most of my coworkers, most of them knew about it anyways). Although I choose to do it only when certain managers are working, I nonetheless count it as a huge victory.

I changed my name legally to Robin Taylor Raynor in 2018. Why did I do this if I'm not going to physically change my gender, you may ask? Well, for one thing, I've always hated the name Tom and Jill gave me and sought to do this for many years before. Also, I wanted to unify my personas. I have every respect for those who can handle more than one name for themselves, but I always found it so tiring!

So what can top all of that, you may ask? How about that I finally found love in my life? First, with the two cats that I adopted (sadly, one is no longer with us), then later on with my first boyfriend. I met him online in a chatroom (I almost didn't, because when he asked to private message me, I clicked on his profile and didn't see much). He was very sweet and gentlemanly, and gave off a good vibe (although I was fortunate to find an honest and sincere person, I caution anyone when dealing with someone online. You never know who's out there.).

We ended up exchanging phone numbers that very day. But when I called him the next night, he didn't answer and I assumed that he had blown me off. Come to find out the next night that a car had hit his bike that day, and he landed in the hospital. During his recovery, and well after that, we've kept in constant contact, and he has come out to CA twice to visit me (he lives in PA).

The long-distance aspect is challenging, but we are currently still together. Maybe the Disney happy ending isn't always a reality, but with all the wonderful people in my life now, it makes me wonder if there's a chance that that's how my life will turn out.

CHAPTER SEVEN

Final Thoughts

Y ou may be wondering why I'm writing this chapter. After all, didn't I describe a happy ending? The reality is that life is not always like that for everyone. Things don't magically fall into place at a certain point in your life. Also, my story is far from over, as I am currently only 46 years old.

The truth is that my road to recovery was paved with a lot of effort, work, and willpower. You should also expect to suffer a setback or two in your journey (God knows I've had my fair share). I also learned during my time in the mental health system in CA that many people have an unrealistic mentality.

"Oh, everything will work itself out if I can just get out of the system and they'd leave me alone...." Not everyone I met in the system is like that, but sadly, many are. I also don't want to give the illusion that I'm out of the system, that I'm miraculously "cured." I still take a great many medications for physical and mental reasons, and I frequently get checked up on.

I guess what I'm trying to get across is that we all have our faults and insecurities. It's how you deal with them that determines if they are a blockade to what you aspire to or desire. If you live in denial like I did for several years, you will most likely never get what you want out of life, and you will be a bitter and miserable little wretch.

The advice I give to you isn't original, but it's tried and true: "Your life is what you make of it." Anything you want is possible, it just boils down to: A) Are you willing to put in the work and effort, and B) Are you willing to do whatever it takes to get it? Most of the time, if you're willing and able, you can have almost anything you want out of life. And even if you don't get exactly what you want, you'll still probably get something out of it.

It really is all up to you in the end.

CPSIA information can be obtained
at www.ICGtesting.com
Printed in the USA
LVHW040915060423
743653LV00024B/765